HOW TO END OUR SPEECH
WITH CONFIDENCE

5 Closing Methods To Finish Like A Pro

MARK DAVIS

Additional copies available by contacting:

Melbourne Education & Training Centre
904/95 Charlotte Street
Brisbane QLD 4000 Australia

Ph: +61-404-178-126

Email Mark@MasterTheArtOfPublicSpeaking.com

Thank you for reading this book.

Here are three quick resources as a gift to you.

#1. Here is a free training audio to help you with your public speaking. Download it now at:

http://www.markdavis.com.au

#2. Get notified when the next new public speaking book is released by subscribing at the website:

http://www.mastertheartofpublicspeaking.com

#3. Public Speaking Mastermind group on Facebook. Join today at:

http://www.facebook.com/groups/publicspeakingmastermind

#3. Finally, if you would like a public speaking workshop in your city, or for your group, contact Coach Mark Davis directly at:

Mark@MasterTheArtOfPublicSpeaking.com

TABLE OF CONTENTS

PREFACE

Closing our speeches professionally is a learned skill.

We can't avoid the end of our presentation. This is where we create our lasting impression, the final soundbite in our audience's mind.

We have to stop talking sometime, so we might as well design the ending of our talk to be effective and memorable.

* Nervous about closing?

* Uncomfortable with asking for a decision?

* Afraid no one will clap?

* Don't know how to finish?

Relax.

Get ready to master five simple and professional ways to quickly and effectively close your talk. All five simple techniques will immediately help us to remove the fear of closing our talk.

Now we can enjoy our public speaking experiences even more. We will walk away from our talks feeling awesome while also achieving our goals.

Caution.

*** This is not a book that covers the entire subject of public speaking. This book only focuses on knowing what to do at the end of our talks! ***

— Mark Davis

The end.

Every speech has to end. Most people do it badly.

Closing well is the payoff.

This is where we:

1. Get the audience to make a decision.

2. Get the audience to take action from our message.

We have to ask ourselves these key questions.

1. Do we want to end with a whimper? Embarrassed because we didn't ask for a decision? Staring at the floor hoping they understood us and liked us?

2. Or, do we want to end with admiration, respect and action from our audience?

The words we choose for the end of our speech will make the difference.

Our presentation is a story.

How will our audience describe our story tomorrow?

Let's look forward in time to our audience's conversation the day after our speech.

Imagine making a cup of coffee or getting a breath of fresh air at the morning break. A colleague comes up and starts this conversation:

"What did you do yesterday?"

"I listened to a presentation on public safety."

"How was it?"

"Boring. Totally wasted 30 minutes of my life."

Ouch. That isn't the impression we want from our audience.

More examples of underwhelming next-day conversations?

"What did you do yesterday?"

"I watched people do a lot of facials and skin treatments."

"How was it?"

"Well, they were pushy, and it seemed from the moment we sat down they were trying to get me to buy something."

Or …

"What did you do yesterday?"

"I went to see an insurance broker."

"How was it?"

"Boring. Too many facts and we left with so much information that we couldn't decide what to do."

Or ...

"What did you do yesterday?"

"I listened to a presentation from the head of the New Environmental Party."

"How was it?"

"Well, I hope he doesn't get elected. Never want to be that bored again."

How about some examples of better conversations?

"What did you do yesterday?"

"I went to a business presentation in the city."

"How was it?"

"Fantastic. They helped me save money on my electricity bill. They even had the paperwork ready to fill in. I saved a bunch of money. I'm going to invest my savings in beer."

Or ...

"What did you do yesterday?"

"I went to a health and nutrition talk."

"How was it?"

"Great. I bought three bottles of their Super Power. I am tired of feeling tired."

Or ...

"What did you do yesterday?"

"I went to buy a car!"

"How was it?"

"Great. The salesman asked my budget, got me to test-drive a few cars, and then worked on getting me a good price. I actually feel good about car salesmen now."

Or ...

"What did you do yesterday?"

"I went to a weight loss workshop."

"How was it?"

"Nice. I learned how to lose weight by changing my breakfast. The good news is that I don't have to join a gym! And I can invest my gym membership savings into more quilting supplies."

What do we want our audience to remember?

Our story. People remember stories. Do we want our audience to remember a good story ... or a bad story?

Well, the good news is that we can manage the story they remember, by controlling how we end our talk.

We don't want our audience to remember or think:

* It was complicated and confusing.

* He was too slick, and all business. No heart.

* It never seemed to end. Too long!

* He cursed, using foul language repeatedly.

* There were 18 speakers and they all blended into one big blur.

* The coffee break was the best part.

* When the speaker turned his back, I ran for the exit.

* I just pretended to enjoy it, but it was bad. I couldn't wait to get out of there.

What experience do we want for our audience?

1. We want our audience to like us. We want to close our talk with positive emotions.

2. We want our audience to see cohesion and connection in our presentation. They should feel our talk was complete.

3. We want our audience to take action. We want to help our audience make a decision.

If we learn to close our talks well, we will jump into the ranks of top performers. Our results will improve and we will be happy to give presentations, knowing that we can close effectively.

The payoff?

* People buy more from salespeople who close well.

* People take action on well-presented causes.

* People invest more with financial planners who can close and offer clear choices.

* People join businesses with people that present clear features and benefits.

* People follow individuals who display clear leadership through their confidence and posture.

* And people love a great punchline from a good joke.

In the business world there are two types of people: The talkers, and the closers. Which one do you want to be?

Memorable endings.

Every talk has to come to an end.

We want our ending to be memorable and to give us the results we desire.

No one wants to finish and be greeted by silence. We want applause.

When we finish, we want the same response that the crowd gives for a goal, a touchdown or a home run.

Or maybe we want an emotional ending, like what we see in the movies.

Remember the movie *Braveheart*, where the British and the Scottish face off in battle?

Motivation by Mel Gibson:

"And dying in your beds, many years from now, would you be willing to trade all the days from this day to that, for one chance, just one chance to tell our enemies, that they may take our lives, but they can never take our freedom!!!!!!" (Cheers from the army, silence from the British.)

Want to inspire and leave a legacy?

A talk from Randy Bausch went viral on YouTube after he announced he would be giving his final lecture due to poor health.

"So today's talk was about my childhood dreams, enabling the dreams of others, and some lessons learned. But it is not about how to achieve your dreams, it is about how to lead your life. If you lead it the right way, karma will take care of itself. The dreams will come to you. And this talk wasn't for you, it was for my family. Thank you all, good night."

Magic kitchen appliance infomercial.

In just a few minutes, a great presenter can sell thousands of dollars' worth of a featured kitchen appliance or tool. Think about it. Yes, the middle of the presentation had great demonstrations, but the ending focused on getting the audience to take action. It may sound something like this:

"We only have 80 of these miracle kitchen aides here at my booth today. And you want to take one of them now while they are on sale, before they are all gone, and you will save shipping and handling too! Just think of your family's happy faces when you prepare your meal this evening with this miracle gadget."

"But wait, there's more!"

The cheesy television infomercials of the 1980s and 1990s used a powerful final statement, which motivated viewers to take immediate action.

"But wait, there's more!" More value and more bonuses made the original price look so amazingly cheap that people couldn't help but say "yes" to the offer. Yes, they had operators standing by to accept the buyers' calls by the thousands.

The final result is action.

We need to create an ending that compels our audience to take actions such as:

* Deciding to buy our product.

* Agreeing to support our cause.

* Joining our business.

* Applauding our presentation, or

* Asking us questions and finding out more.

This book will show you exactly how to do that. When the end of our talk is well-planned and well-executed, it will be remembered and talked about!

Now we can sell more, grow our business faster, convince more people, and make more friends.

The five closes.

**There are five simple ways to close your talk
in this book.**

1. Closes that are focused on decisions and actions.

2. Quick, 20-second closes for the times when we have to finish fast.

3. Closes that trigger feelings and emotions in our audience.

4. Professional, logical, systematic closes.

5. Instructional closes that tell the audience what to do next.

**We will learn how to do each of these closings
for our talks.**

So first, a few quick reasons why we must close our speeches professionally.

Reason #1: Results.

The biggest difference between a good ending and a bad one is the result.

* In sales, it is the dollar value of products we sell.

* In insurance, it is the policy value we have negotiated when we finish the phone call.

* In network marketing, it is a new distributor committing to join.

* In a staff meeting, it is getting our desired strategy into action.

* In the world of relationships, it is getting someone to return your call.

* At a wedding, it is having the crowd cheer loudly, drink the toast, and respect and admire your speech with feedback all night.

* In a political speech, it is getting the audience to take action to contact their family and friends to vote for you.

Regardless of whether people are giving us applause, buying products or giving us a score out of 10, we need to have our speech neatly wrapped up. This will complement a good opening and a well-presented talk.

Reason #2: Resolution.

In the beginning of our speech, we might set up a problem, question or argument that is the focus of our talk.

To get the best close out of our talk, we need to resolve our opening during our closing comments.

The human mind doesn't like open, unresolved issues. We don't want our audience to leave our talk feeling as though we just talked about challenges, yet offered no solutions. They won't tell their friends a very good story about their experience.

Our audience wants completion. They want to hear the challenges we present and our solutions.

Opening and closing examples.

The opening sentences and the closing sentences are the bookends of our talk. They should match. This helps make a logical "sandwich" for people.

The audience loved our opening sentences. They enjoy the substance of our speech in the middle of our presentation. And now, they want our ending sentences to wrap up the whole talk neatly in their minds. Are we up to it? Of course.

Here are two easy guidelines to remember.

#1. The opening sentences of our talk suggests an action or a decision, and the closing sentences asks for that action or decision.

#2. Keeping the opening and closing similar is why the conclusion may sound like a summary. Key points that are set out in the beginning are repeated in the close. We can't expect our audience to clearly remember our opening sentences.

Opening/Closing Example #1.

Opening sentence: "We are here today to discover the fastest way to make money in the current market. We will do this without property, shares or high-capital investment."

Closing sentence: "We discovered today the fastest way to make money in the current market. Having our own online home-based business is possible for everyone here. That is why we should register online now."

Opening/Closing Example #2.

Opening sentence: "How many people wish they had more youthful-looking skin, but don't want a complicated beauty routine?"

Closing sentence: "Today, we discovered how applying Wonder Night Cream every evening makes our skin younger while we sleep. So instead of us lying in bed listening to our skin wrinkle at night, we now have a solution to keep those wrinkles away. Please think of others when you leave here today. Of course, get a jar of Wonder Night Cream for yourself, but maybe you can bring one extra jar home for your mother or close friend."

Opening/Closing Example #3.

Opening sentence: "What can I say to honor my best friend who is married today?"

Closing sentence: "So what can I say to honor my best friend who is married today? I wish to say that everyone here at the reception appreciates the joy you have brought into our lives. So to honor you, can we all stand and give a toast to my best friend and his lovely bride?"

As we can see, the closing sentences give completion to our speech when we mirror our opening statement. Easy to do, and our audience appreciates how we made our message easy to digest.

So we can look at how we opened our speech, and just put most of those same words into our closing statement. The simplest finish ever.

But how do we know when it is the right time to close or finish our speech?

So "when" and "how" should we finish our speech?

What?

Yes, this book is about how to close our speeches, so our audience takes action: to buy, to commit, to agree with our message.

However, if we don't finish our speech at the right time, our audience will be turned off before our closing comments even begin.

Let me tell you about Jim.

Jim was delivering his 45-minute presentation. After 35 minutes, he announces to the audience, "Okay, I just finished Point #1. I have six more points I wanted to cover. I will speed up and try to do as many as I can in the next ten minutes."

How do you think the audience reacted? They groaned.

Jim was already talking so fast they couldn't take notes. And now, they just found out they were going to get just a fraction of the information he promised.

21

The audience felt ripped off. They gave up trying to pay attention. So, they turned to their phones to see what was happening in the rest of the world.

When he finally finished, he was overtime by 10 minutes and everyone knew he wasn't anywhere near the end of his talk.

Jim could have simply finished with point number one, and the audience would have been happy. And none the wiser.

He made the mistake of planting a negative seed in the mind of the crowd. That was their final impression, and all the good work of his presentation disappeared.

The best time to close and finish our talk?

When we announce we are finished, and before our time limit is up!

There is an old saying, "Timing is everything!" This is true with presentations.

Nobody cares if our talk finishes early, but everybody will judge us harshly if we talk past our assigned time. Knowing when to finish our talk is our first step to setting up our closing message.

The simplest and safest rule: Finish early or on time.

Look professional.

Being disorganized, Jim didn't look professional. He gave the appearance of being unprepared, which is disrespectful to his audience.

He didn't plan his talk properly. Chances are he never did a dress rehearsal for his speech. Maybe he didn't think his audience was important enough to invest the time to prepare properly.

Jim thought he could "wing it" and fill in the gaps with his witty chatter.

We must plan our talks to finish early. Why? Because it is common courtesy to the host and the audience.

It is easy to add an extra few sentences or points to our talk if we do have extra time. However, it is very difficult to cut out important points in our talks when our time is cut short.

So as a professional, let's plan for the unexpected. Let's have our speech constructed to finish early if needed. And do our best parts first!

Another reason we might have to finish early.

Lunch? If we speak just before lunch we might notice our audience doing things like:

* Fidgeting in their chairs.

* Looking at their phones.

* Making paper airplanes.

* Drawing pictures on their notes.

* Whispering to their friends.

* Looking at the ceiling.

* Looking at the door!

* Falling asleep!

Or, maybe the audience is waiting for a break, the next speaker, or a chance to leave early. There are many reasons outside of our control why our audience may have finished listening, but we haven't finished talking.

At that point it is time to use a short and effective close to finish our talk quickly.

Announcing we are ready to finish.

We can relax our audience by giving a signal that we will finish our talk shortly. This takes away the drama inside of their heads. They won't be thinking, "How much longer is this going to last? When will it be over? Should I just sneak out now?"

The audience appreciates the signal that we give them that we will finish shortly. Consider this as warming up the audience for our close.

If our audience knows we are finishing shortly, they can then listen closely to our closing words. That is what we want.

But first, let's be practiced and professional. We can't just finish our talk by saying, "Okay, I'm done! Bye!" That looks so ... awful.

The audience expects a great close. We would disappoint them with the "Okay, I'm done! Bye!" finish to our talk.

**Here are some examples of how to prepare our
audience for our closing message.**

* "My final story for tonight ..."

* "One last story to leave you with tonight ..."

* "The final thing I would like to share with you ..."

* "In conclusion, this story wraps up ..."

* "This will give us all an inspiring finish ..."

* "The best way to finish tonight is with my favorite
story."

* "So we have about 10 minutes until we finish today.
Time to review what we have discussed ..."

* "The hotel is going to come in and start packing away
the chairs in about 15 minutes, so time to review ..."

* "And finally, Point #10 in our 10-point checklist ..."

**Now the audience knows to pay attention,
as the conclusion will offer:**

1. A special offer you might be selling.

2. A message you would like them to remember.

3. A decision they need to make.

4. An action you would like them to take.

5. A cue to start their applause.

More statements to announce you are about to finish.

There are many great lead-up statements to notify our audience that we are about to finish, such as:

* "So, in closing ..."

* "Now, the final question is ..."

* "Without further ado ..."

* "The last thing I'd like to mention ..."

These are natural lead-up statements.

What others could we use to professionally let our audience know the end is coming?

Time.

* "In ten minutes, we will be finishing ..."

* "In five minutes, I'm going to ask you a question about which product you like the most."

* "In seven minutes, we are going to take a break."

* "In 20 minutes, you will be in your car ..."

* "In one hour, you will be home ..."

* "In three minutes, we will be wrapping up."

* "In six minutes, I will be offering you 6 choices ..."

* "In two minutes, I will be finished and ready for questions."

* "In ten minutes, I can take your questions ..."

Warnings.

* "Don't be surprised when we finish soon and ..."

* "Don't be alarmed, we are going to finish on time."

* "We will get you out of here very soon and on your way."

* "Be prepared for the special offer I'm about to share with you at the end."

* "You will want to pay attention to this final wrap-up."

* "I have to warn you ... this ending is going to get ugly."

* "I want to tell you there is a big decision for you to make now."

* "I have a special offer coming up in just a few minutes."

* "I am going to ask you a question when we close."

* "Now I will do what you fear most ... try and sell you something."

* "I am about to ask you what kind of commitment you will make."

* "I am about to put the decision for your child's future in your hands."

* "I am going to have to make you an offer you can't refuse."

* "Have I got some choices for you? Yes, here are the three options to get started."

Notifying other people.

* "Can someone prepare the host? I am about to finish in two minutes."

* "Is the next speaker ready? Because I am about finished with these slides."

* "Now would the award winners start lining up on the left as we are about to announce ..."

* "Don't stretch yet, as we are almost finished."

* "What time is it? Okay, good. Because we are close to the finish line."

Finish on time.

The benefits of finishing on time?

1. It allows us enough time to deliver our message.

2. It will get our audience to pay attention to our closing words and message.

3. It gives us the opportunity for a successful talk, but we must still deliver with a professional close.

So let's jump into the five closes that will give us the best possible final impression with our audience.

The five closes we can use.

Yes, one size or one type of close doesn't fit every situation. Here are some variables we might consider:

* What type of audience are we speaking to?

* What is the environment? A large auditorium or a noisy restaurant?

* What is the final outcome we desire? A sale? Applause? An action?

* Does the audience know me, or am I a stranger?

* If my presentation is to the board of directors, do they just want the facts?

* Do I want my audience to feel a motivational high when I finish?

* How do I want to be remembered?

How do we make decisions about all of these different situations?

Good judgment.

Good judgment comes from preparation and experience.

For example:

* A long-winded close to the parents of the local school, who just want to get home to prepare for work tomorrow. Bad experience.

* A high-pressure manipulative close to social workers to be more efficient. Bad experience.

* A close asking for action to help the community build a park. Good experience.

* A close giving the audience a chance to enroll in a course starting tomorrow. Good experience.

Not prepared? Not respecting the audience's expectations? Well, we will leave a poor final impression.

Prepared? Meeting our audience's expectations? We will be remembered fondly.

If we need to refer to our notes, for pricing, product names, package deals - we will look unprofessional and unprepared.

Planning and preparation will make us look professional. However, we still need to say something when we close.

Our ending sentences can take these five paths to close our presentation:

1. Closes that are decision- and action-focused.

2. Quick, 20-second closes for the times when we have to close fast.

3. Closes that trigger feelings and emotions in our audience.

4. Professional, logical, systematic closes.

5. Instructional closes that tell the audience what to do next.

Let's learn how to do these five techniques now.

Decisions.

Our audience will make up their mind ... every time. As professionals, we want them to make a decision that is clear and actionable.

Easy decisions first.

Let's start with some easy ways you could close your talk and ask for a decision. Ready?

* "So what do you think?"

* "Well, those are the three options. Which option suits you best?"

* "We can get you started today, is that okay?"

* "All those in favor of this proposal, please raise your hands. All those who are not in favor, please raise your hands. This proposal passes by a vote of 7 to 3."

* "Thank you for your attention today. What would you like to do next?"

* "Getting started immediately is possible for the first three people who raise their hands."

* "And now, the rest is up to you."

And now, for the audience, it is "decision time." They must focus on what action they will take next.

Why get that decision?

Salesmen get paid on orders. They don't get paid by the word count of their presentations.

Network marketers get paid to build an organization of distributors. They don't get paid for the time they spend with prospects.

Real estate agents get paid for selling a home. They don't get paid for the mileage for showing homes.

Politicians know they won't get elected unless they convince volunteers to knock on doors and solicit more voters.

Salesmen know that unless they get an application, contract, or order form in front of a customer, nothing is going to happen. Having a professional ending to any presentation makes that possible.

Not a salesperson?

What if you are trying to encourage the school council to put in safer playground equipment? You need to get action. The end of your talk is the time to ask for action.

At the end of your wedding speech, with everyone staring at you, holding their champagne in the air, you have to close with action. What do you say? "Let's toast the bride and groom now. Cheers!"

Everyone knows the action to take!

When we offer clear choices, it is easy for the audience to make a decision. This lowers the focus on us, and puts all of the pressure on the audience. Now they have to decide what action they will take.

Give the audience permission.

When the audience has permission to act, they often do. People spend a lot of their life surrounded by rules that say what they can't do. Give them permission and you just might find more people say yes and take positive action.

"You can ..."

1. "When I finish this talk in two minutes' time, you can leave right away ... or you can put your chair against the wall, then walk outside for a snack and a drink that we have prepared for you. By the way, the cookies are delicious."

2. "When I finish, here is what you can do next. Go talk to someone in the back of the room for further information on how you can get started. Or, if you have questions, come to the front and talk to me. I will answer your questions."

3. "When I finish here, you can get started right away by filling out the form on your table. Just start at the top where it says name, and write your name."

4. "When I finish this speech, you can go home and start to write your business plan. By tomorrow morning, you will have your 12-month plan for action."

5. "When I finish talking in about two minutes, you can decide to continue living as you have in the past. Or, you could visit with me before you leave, and talk to me about the changes you are ready to make."

6. "When the talk finishes in ten minutes, you can ask me a question, fill in the order form, or log on and subscribe to the email updates."

7. "When you leave today, you can start writing a list of prospective customers for this product. Who do you know that wants to look younger and have more energy?"

Ask for questions.

1. "When I finish this talk, I would like to open it up for questions. If you have been thinking about what to ask, now is the time to gather your questions."

2. "When I finish here tonight, you can come forward and ask me a personal question."

3. "When we finish this webinar, you can text or email me your personal questions. I will do my best to answer your question within 24 hours."

You can ... register online.

1. "When I finish in three minutes' time, you can pull out your smartphone. Then go to this website and register for free right away!"

2. "You can fill in your details at this website immediately. Then you will get a free report on how to make $10,000 in the next three months."

3. "You can get a free gift with your order if you register tonight."

Goals.

1. "This goal-setting seminar is over. But before I finish, it is time for you to write a list of three goals you want to achieve in the next seven days. This will give you action steps. I have already given you the motivation!"

2. "Now that we are finished, you can write down the name of the three vacation spots you will visit when you are successful with this venture. Be sure to include ones that you can take your spouse to!"

Try a sample.

1. "If you are excited about this product, that is great. Because as soon as we finish this talk, we have some free samples waiting in the back of the room. Be sure to try both the chocolate and vanilla flavors!"

2. "Thanks for coming. Be sure to get a copy of the brochure which will show you a sample of the bathroom tiles, feature walls and furniture. This could be what your new property will look like."

Start writing.

1. "When we finish tonight, you can go home and write the first 1,000 words of your book. It will take one hour. You will go to sleep knowing you are taking action towards your writing goal!"

2. "You have the tools now to write amazing headlines. Before you go, you can test your new knowledge. Write down five new headlines you imagine could be on the front page of the newspaper tomorrow."

"Over to you!"

Another action or decision close is to pass the responsibility to the audience to act. We have now given them permission to take action. This puts the ball back in the audience's court for a decision.

When we give people the responsibility to make a decision themselves, they feel empowered. No pressure is coming from us.

Can we close our talk this quickly? Of course we can.

"Over to you - would you like to start today or next week?"

"Over to you - red or black?"

"Over to you - small, medium or large?"

"Over to you - any questions?"

"Over to you - the order form is in front of you. Start at the top with your name."

"Over to you - the person sitting with you can answer any final questions you might have."

"Over to you - choose the next chairman by casting your vote."

Want a few more?

"Over to you - download the app and create your free account now!"

"Over to you - VIP Membership is open for the next 10 minutes."

"Over to you - you can decide to join or not."

"Over to you - time to start traveling and see the world now!"

"Over to you - time to start writing that book right now!"

"Over to you - what do you think?"

"Over to you - it is up to you."

More responsibility for them. Less pressure on us.

It is up to them to buy or not buy. Join or don't join. Say yes or no.

With lower-pressure closes like this, you can let them convince themselves. Plus, we will have a lot less "buyer's remorse" when they make the decision for themselves. Here are a few examples.

1. "That is all I have to say about myself and my questions about the job. It is up to you. Can you see me fitting in here or not? It is up to you to take advantage of my skills and experience and hire me ... or not."

2. "It is up to you, everything I know, you now know too. If you would like to get started, great. But nobody will twist your arm. The decision is yours."

3. "That is it! The rest is up to you. The vitamins won't work unless you take them daily. Get a pack and start taking them tonight."

"Be the first."

There is always someone in the audience that loves to be first. The first to buy, the first to try. If they like what they hear, they enjoy being the first to commit.

We can close our talk by talking to this need.

Think we can come up with a few ways to include some "firsts" in our close? Of course.

What do people want to be first at?

Be the first to try the product.

Be the first to get your book autographed.

Be the first ticketholder.

Be the first to share a photo.

Be the first to register for the workshop.

Be the first to volunteer.

Be the first to stand up.

Be the first to do an exercise.

Be the first to get their credit card out.

Be the first to save money.

Be the first to open their own business.

Be the first to take control of their taxes.

Be the first to get insurance tailored to their needs.

Be the first to try a sample.

Be the first to get a makeover.

Be the first to get a massage.

Be the first out the door.

Be the first to pose for a photo with the speaker.

Be the first on stage!

We can offer them the chance to be the first at any of these things, and the close is done! Simple, quick, and rejection-free.

Save money.

What else do people like to make decisions on? Saving money.

Using the word "save" makes it irresistible for natural-born shoppers. Do you have a good offer? Then suggest how much they can save by making a decision today.

Salespeople that work in retail use this every day, because they know a customer only comes past once. If they don't get the sale, one of the hundreds of other stores will get the customer's money.

Some examples of using "savings" in your close.

Save $100 now.

Save $3,879 this year by acting now.

Save $4 off your parking.

Save $99 - Buy one, get one free!

Save over $1,000!

Save by buying in bulk.

Save by buying 3, getting 1 free.

Save by accessing the sales items online.

Save with our Christmas Sale online.

Save with this rebate from the government.

Save with this $100 cash-back offer.

Save with instant cash-back in store!

Getting the hang of this? What else do people want to do?

Take things home.

If people like to be first, to save, and to make their own decisions, what else do they like to do at the end of a talk?

Think about special events like conferences, conventions and trade shows. They always have samples. People feel they have more value in any experience when they take away more than they arrived with.

Ready for some examples?

"When you walk out of here tonight…"

You can take home a sample of the product.

You can take home a sample of the diet shake.

You can take home a sample of the coffee.

You can take home a sample of the skin cream.

You can take home my business card.

You can take home your notes, ideas and memories.

You can take home a photo of us together on stage.

You can take home a set of all five books, audios and videos.

You can take home a bargain.

You can take home the deal of a lifetime.

You can take home your reservation details.

You can take home your appointment card.

You can take home your schedule of coaching sessions.

You can take home your list of to-do items.

You can take home the plans for the new apartment.

You can take home the prospectus for the investment.

Some of our audience will just leave. We can't stop them.

What about those audience members that stay? How about a closing statement to encourage them to hang around, giving you more time to communicate and bond with them?

"When we finish, you can stay ..."

You can stay and have a photo with me.

You can stay and ask more questions.

You can stay and try a sample.

You can stay and meet with our product expert.

You can stay and discuss our business model.

You can stay and fill in the paperwork.

You can stay and chat to your friends.

You can stay and eat some snacks.

You can stay and talk with our staff.

You can stay and review the choices for starting in the business.

You can stay and try out the technology we were using.

You can stay and write a list of friends you would like to refer to us.

Want more ways to give your audience permission?

"It is okay for you ..."

It is okay for you to try as many products as you like.

It is okay for you to start your business tonight.

It is okay for you to go home and think about it.

It is okay for you to stay here and have a party with us.

It is okay for you to register for the next training session.

It is okay for you to leave your email address with the registration table.

It is okay for you to buy a few books for yourself and someone else.

It is okay to ask for an autograph for a friend.

Sometimes people want to get a good deal. You can work that into your final closing sentence. Good deals get their attention, and get action.

"So the deal is ..."

You join today and I help you earn $1,000 a week part-time.

You buy today and get a 20% boost in energy instantly.

You buy today and look 15 years younger overnight.

You buy today and save the 7% stamp duty of more than $20,000.

You buy today and get the preferred customer rate saving you $1,700.

The secret weapon of time.

We can use past, present and future to get the audience to act now! Time is one of our most precious resources. So we can use it in our closes to get people to take action.

By using references to the past, the present and the future, we can bring people into the present to make a decision now. We can create the urgency for our audience to make a decision. Or, we can suggest a low-pressure approach and let the audience work it out for themselves.

The past.

When people look back, they often blame themselves for bad decisions. This affects their willingness to move forward and to make a choice to act. We can reassure our audience by acknowledging the value of the past. Then we can reframe decisions in the present moment.

Some examples?

"When we look back, not every investment made us money. But, we learned along the way. Now it is easier to make better choices when we look at properties to buy."

"When we look to the past, we romanticize how great our decisions were. But, we forget how luck played a big part. We can't predict luck. However, we can start creating our own luck now by moving forward."

"Hindsight is 20/20. If we could go back in time, there would be some things we would change. But, we can't change the past. We can only learn from it."

How about specific moments in time?

"If we look back three months, we didn't have these products to choose from. New and improved formulas are now available. You can be the first to get access to them. You are in the right place at the right time tonight."

"If we look back three months, we couldn't have known the director would resign. But here we are now, needing to appoint a new director to the company. So, we need to vote now. Please write the name of your nomination and put it in the box as we pass it around."

Further back?

"This time last year, if you looked at your credit card statement, was it better or worse than it is now? Has anything changed? If it is time to make it better and remove that credit card debt, then it is time to get started in this business."

"One year ago I was standing right here. Only 15 people were in the room listening to me talk about the Wonder Product. Now, 150 people are here and I want to thank you all for coming. Thank you for your interest in the latest formula. We have your free samples. Come on up!"

"One year ago I was unemployed, single, and living in my mother's spare room at the age of 33. Today I am earning a great income with my business. I just bought my own house! I am glad I can be here to share how I did it with you tonight. Thanks for listening."

Across generations, we can make even broader statements.

"In the 1980s, the first microwave ovens came out. Before that we cooked on the stove or in the oven. Thanks to advances in technology, we can now do amazing things like make popcorn in 90 seconds.

"Even more amazing are the things we can do with nutritious meals. You have seen the demonstrations, now it is time to place your order."

More phrases to start our final sentence referring to the past.

The other day …

Three days ago …

Last week …

Last night …

10 years ago …

20 years ago …

100 years ago …

**The future is a great topic to focus on
when we close a talk.**

"When you leave here, energized and enthusiastic, you will want to tell others about this. Do it online! Share how you feel in a quick 10-second video. Your friends and family will know you are on fire!"

"When you leave, you will have made a business decision that will improve product sales. This is an investment into your business growth. Now you can hire more staff, have new offices, and make more money every month!"

More examples.

"When you leave, you will have the key to making more money."

"When you leave, you will have the secret to opening your presentations effectively."

"When you leave, you will have the secret to closing a talk effectively."

"When you leave, you will have the skills to create effective Facebook Ads."

"When you leave, you will have the outline for your first book."

"When you leave, you will be able to make eye contact with your customers."

"When you leave, you will have the secret to great customer service in your business."

"When you leave, you will have the strategy for coaching your team to success."

"When you leave, you will have the tools to build a championship team."

"When you leave, you will be confident to try new things."

"When you leave, you will be able to talk to people older than you."

"When you leave, you will be able to find anything on your phone."

"When you leave, you will have the taste of our super juice in your mind."

"When you leave, you will know you got the best deal."

"When you leave, you will have a business plan for the future."

"When you leave, you will have the knowledge you need to succeed."

Tomorrow endings.

"Tomorrow, you will wake up with more energy than ever. You will have a clear direction and the motivation to achieve your goals."

"Tomorrow, you will be taking the first steps on the journey to success in your business. You will have a strategy and the direction to take you forward."

"Tomorrow, you will see the wrinkles start to fade."

"Tomorrow, you will have more energy."

"Tomorrow, you will be drinking your morning coffee knowing it is good for you."

"Tomorrow, you will open your computer and write your first chapter."

"Tomorrow, you will look at your smartwatch and it will look awesome on your wrist."

"Tomorrow, you will look in the mirror and see a beautiful smile."

"Tomorrow, you will put your hands together and be amazed at how soft they feel."

"Tomorrow, you will take your vitamins and feel great."

"Tomorrow, you will work all day and still have the energy to entertain your in-laws at dinner."

"Tomorrow, you will work all day and want to work more!"

"Tomorrow, you will work all day and still write all night."

Next week endings.

Next week sounds realistic. You can make the future look easier to achieve by giving them more time.

Some examples?

"Next week, you will hop on the scales and be happy. You will be three pounds lighter!"

"Next week, you will have mastered your new phone and be downloading apps like a teenager."

"Next week, you will have written over 5,000 words in your book."

"Next week, you will be meeting new people to talk to about this business."

"Next week, you will have spoken to 10 new prospects and handed out 10 samples."

"Next week, you will have new customers happy to give you testimonials."

"Next week, you will have five new reviews on TripAdvisor."

Give them more time to visualize success.
In three months …

"In three months' time, you will have lost 20 pounds! You will have the energy levels of a teenager and will feel like you can do anything!"

"When you look back in three months, you will be seeing more money in your PayPal account. Why? Because you practiced the three key strategies of successful online marketers."

"In three months, you will be giving talks in front of 100 people … and earning money doing it!"

"In three months, you will have better staff productivity by introducing weekly three-minute massages. It will be the favorite day of the week. People will be begging to come and work for you!"

"In three months' time, we will review the budget again. We will see where these agreed-upon changes have improved our bottom line."

The present endings.

Focusing on the present is important when we want people to take action. Thinking about the past or future won't help when we need to get action now.

"Today we have looked at three ways to start making money right away. You can take advantage of this news by registering to sell this product and make 30% retail profit. We look forward to working with you."

"Today we have presented the business model we distribute our products and services through. It is not a new method. However, our way of sharing the profits with our team is powerful and proven. I look forward to working with you."

"Right now there is nothing more I can say. We have presented the budget for the next six months and have answered the questions. I submit to the board that we accept the budget and agree to work towards achieving the savings now."

"Tonight is the perfect time to start losing weight. You see how the product works. You heard from people who successfully lost 5 to 15 pounds in just one month. You also know how to get your product for free by introducing four new customers. Let's get started!"

Beginning words to start your closing.

Today …

Tonight …

Right now …

Immediately after we finish …

In this moment …

On this day …

Here at this workshop …

Here in this boardroom …

Right away …

Now you can …

Now you will see …

By now you know …

By now you want …

By now you are ready …

You are ready …

You are prepared …

You are set to go …

How To End Our Speech
With Confidence

You are okay to start …

You have done all you need to do …

No more wasting time …

No more delaying …

No more wondering …

This is the right time …

This is the best time …

This is a good time …

This is your time …

This is our time …

This is the first day of the rest of your life …

This is the first day of your adventure …

This is the first day of work …

This is the first day of freedom …

And finally, "Yes. No. Or not right now."

Quick closes in 20 seconds or less.

Yes, it is possible to finish your talk in less than 20 seconds.

How much writing equals 20 seconds of talking? About 50 words. About four sentences, not much at all.

In that short time, we can prepare a few sentences that will make us look professional when we close.

For a quick close, try using reminders, questions, assumptions and introductions.

Reminders.

One way to close quickly is to "remind" the audience of something.

1. Remind them of the benefit of your product.

"So as we have discovered, the key focus for our immune system to be at optimal defense level is the X vitamin. Get enough of it and we function at 100%. If we don't get enough, our health suffers. The vitamin is $29.95 per bottle and we have bottles at the back of the room!"

***

"Just a reminder for everyone as we close. The miracle ingredient in this shampoo will make hair grow blonde from roots to tips within three weeks. You can change to the red, brunette or black miracle shampoo at any time for the same results. Bottles are $14.95 each."

***

"The key ingredient in our formula for investing success is a team of researchers. All day, every day, they are scanning the investment world for properties. So then you can buy, flip and sell for a 30% profit. You get access to that team when you join our syndicate today."

2. Remind them of the deadline.

"I would like to remind you that the special offer for just $197 is only available today. You can take advantage of it now. We have paperwork to help you get started immediately. Peter is here to answer any questions and to help process your payment."

***

"I would like to remind you that this is the first showing of our business in Singapore. If you are joining us today, there are bonuses. They include: the full-day training, two-for-one product bonus, and 10 mentoring sessions. You are in first! So you are in the elite leader group with extra bonuses."

***

"Just a quick reminder that the deadline for the sales promotion we have discussed is this Friday! Qualify for the bonus by selling an extra three boxes of product between now and then. All bonus winners go into the drawing for a free trip to Vegas!"

3. Remind them when you have another talk.

"So that is all we have time for today. I will be back on Thursday at 7pm for another conference call. We will discuss the three secrets to getting multiple streams of income. Be sure to invite your friends and colleagues."

***

"As we finish, I would like you to put in your diary the date of next week's networking event. It is at the Radisson City Center. Start time is at 3pm followed by cocktails at 6pm. RSVP online through the registration page. We will see you there!"

***

"Finishing up now, I would like to remind you of my next talk. Tomorrow I will be at the Marriott Hotel doing a follow-up presentation. Anyone that wants to come along can register at the website or text me. We will reserve your spot."

4. Remind them why you were there.

"It has been a pleasure to be with you today to show you the three ways to create property investment income. I hope the way forward looks clear for your financial independence. I know we can find a path that works for you."

***

"I am happy I could be here tonight to outline the details of our new nutraceutical line. You have seen the difference from other companies' vitamin supplements. You've also seen saw how you can make money retailing and promoting our line. So who would like to come on the journey of sharing these products with the world?"

***

"You welcomed me here today and I appreciate it. I want to remind you that I am here at the invitation of the leaders. They wanted to provide you with the skills to be successful in your businesses. Now you have some more business-building techniques to help you grow faster. I wish you all the best."

5. Remind them of your contact details.

"You can email me at my personal email address, mark@markdavis.com.au anytime. My phone number is +61-404-178-126. You are welcome to contact me. Thanks for coming!"

***

"As we close, please be sure to write down the customer service information. Our email and phone number is on the slide behind me. It is okay for you to take a photo of this slide or enter it into your phone now."

***

"We have offices around the country, and your closest office is right here at 123 Main Street. It is open 9am-5pm. We look forward to having you come in to view the hotel suites. You can get a taste of how you will feel when you invest with us."

6. Remind them what is happening next.

"Our next speaker is a legend. She has done amazing things in this area and has over 17 years' experience. You will learn the latest breakthroughs and the most recent announcements. Thank you for your time and please welcome our next speaker, Mrs. Z!"

***

"Coming up next is the best part ... our break! During our break, you can come up and ask me a question, get your book signed, and get a cup of coffee or water. The break is also a great time to stretch, so everyone please stand up! Enjoy your break!"

***

"After the break, we will be discussing the best ways to create buzz in your sales team. Every manager will want to be here and take plenty of notes. This presentation has increased sales up to 57% when the ideas are implemented. See you after the break!"

We can also remind them about key topics that are relevant to them. This maintains rapport and gives them something else to thank us for.

We can remind them to:

* Drive home safely.

* Turn their phone back on.

* Call the babysitter.

* Text their wife or husband.

How To End Our Speech
With Confidence

* Pick up their product samples.

* Fill in the order form.

* Hand in their business card.

* Get their parking validated.

* Get on the free mailing list.

Questions.

When we close quickly by asking a question, we provide the audience with a point to focus on.

Their energy and attention is on answering our question. And, after answering our question, they will feel good about our talk.

Questions will give them the chance to agree, disagree, or make a decision.

Here are some suggestions for effective questions you can use for your close.

Who, What, Which, When, Where, Why or How.

***

"Who."

When we ask "Who," the audience has to think of a real person. The audience has to put a face they know into the answer. It might be them, or someone they know. However, they can't leave the question unanswered, even if the answer is, "I don't know."

Some examples?

How To End Our Speech
With Confidence

"Who do you think is the most likely person to be successful? The person who did not come tonight? Or you, the person who made the commitment to come?"

***

"Who here can see that this insurance has the best coverage? We offer lower pricing, fantastic customer service and a free iPad. So let's get you started by filling in this form."

***

"Who is the person that needs this product the most in this room? The healthy one? The unfit one? Or any person wanting to change their life? Let's get you started right now and meet the goals you have."

***

* "Who feels more confident about their presentation now?"

* "Who knows what they want to do in their business?"

* "Who has found the best product mix for them to sell?"

* "Who has an online strategy for finding new customers?"

* "Who wants to be the first to take advantage of this great deal tonight?"

* "Who will be the first to get to Diamond?"

* "Who is ready to begin right now?"

* "Who wants to take minutes at the next meeting?"

"What."

"What" is an opener for specifics. It is a question that must get a response, and is great for actions or choices. Examples?

"What is the best product in our range? The product that solves your problem right now. What about our other products? You can take home the catalog and order additional products later!"

***

"What did you hope to discover by coming here today? Was it the miracle solution for your skin? The secret to more energy? The trick to losing weight? I hope you have your answers. And if you didn't get the solution you were looking for, visit with me personally when we finish."

***

"What is going to be different when you walk out the door? Your dreams of financial freedom? Or your leadership skills to make a difference in the lives of many?"

***

"What do you think?"

This is low pressure. And that is why your audience will appreciate this polite ending. Plus, when we stop talking, we let your audience tell us exactly what they think!

When we ask for an opinion, we just might get the truth! Use any of these closing lines to create your own 20-second close.

* "What do you think?"

* "What do you think about the products?"

* "What do you think about being in your own business?"

* "What do you think about working your own part-time business?"

* "What do you think about making more money?"

* "What do you think about living on the beach?"

* "What do you think about retiring before you are 40?"

* "What do you think about leaving the world of full-time work?"

* "What do you think about the idea of writing your own book?"

* "What do you think about the investment?"

* "What do you think about the opportunity?"

* "What do you think about traveling more now?"

* "What do you think about seeing the world?"

* "What do you think about these tax-reduction strategies?"

* "What do you think about building an international business?"

* "What do you think about getting paid even while you are asleep?"

* "What do you think about the options presented?"

"Which."

When you offer a choice, they have to make a decision! Which one should they pick? Well, the good news is that when they pick one of the options, they have made a choice. No more "thinking it over" and delaying their decision.

"Which of these options is the best for you? The big package that gets you one of everything? The middle package with three of the top selling products? Or one product that will address your biggest health challenge right now?"

***

"Which investment sounds like the best one for you? The conservative bricks-and-mortar property complex? Or the more volatile stocks and shares portfolio? Which choice excites you more?"

* "Which product will help you lose weight faster, the Shake or Cleanse?"

* "Which product do you see helping your hair type best, Lavender or Chamomile?"

* "Which product do you want to focus on first, Energy or Stress?"

* "Which is more important to your family, airbags or engine size?"

* "Which airline do you like to fly, A or B?"

* "Which day of the week would you prefer to fly, Monday or Friday?"

* "Which day do you want to meet for our review, Tuesday or Thursday?"

* "Which Caribbean destination do you prefer, Jamaica or Trinidad?"

* "Which color suits your office best, blue or purple?"

* "Which seminar will help you most in your profession, Public Speaking or Time Management?"

* "Which frequent traveler program do you want to add to your booking, hotel or airline?"

* "Which credit card would you like to use, Visa or MasterCard?"

"When."

"When" questions get people thinking about a moment in time. It is a specific question, but we can also use it to get an answer that is "now!"

"When do you want things to change? Is it going to be today that you start your own business? Start the journey to having a second income to help you retire in the next five years. When is the best time to take your first step?"

***

"When do we schedule the next board meeting? The Friday before Christmas, or the first Friday in the New Year? Can we get an agreement, please? All in favor of Christmas, show of hands. New Year? New Year it is."

***

"When will John and Jane finish their honeymoon? John told me, 'Never.' He said that when they land back home, their passion will keep them happy and united forever. We wish them all the best. Here is our toast to the happy couple, John and Jane!"

***

* "When do you want to quit your job?"

* "When do you want to retire?"

* "When do you want to start your own business?"

* "When will you be able to jump in and grow something for yourself?"

* "When do you see yourself taking control of your destiny?"

* "When will you take responsibility for your future?"

* "When will you be able to act on your dreams?"

* "When will the future be more important than the past?"

* "When will the price be right?"

* "When will the time be right?"

* "When will you propose?"

* "When will you give up?"

* "When will you start writing?"

* "When will you have your own website?"

* "When are you going to publish a blog?"

* "When will you have an email newsletter for your customers?"

* "When will you have enough money to retire?"

* "When will the credit card debt be gone?"

* "When is a good time to pay less in taxes?"

* "When do you see your investments including property?"

* "When do you want to get started working for us?"

* "When can you send your invoice through?"

* "When can you arrive?"

* "When can you start?"

"Where."

"Where" can be a place, a mindset, or a conceptual location.

"Where do you want to go in your business? Is today the day you move in a new direction, towards the top? Is today the day you move ahead with your first step?"

***

"Is this the day you stop making the same mistakes in life? Are you ready for a total U-turn?"

***

"Where is the ideal location for your next vacation? We can help you get to that vacation fast."

***

* "Where do you see yourself in five years?"

* "Where do you see your motivation coming from?"

* "Where do you feel you want to focus your business strategy?"

* "Where will you find new prospects when you leave here?"

* "Where are you going to find your first three prospects?"

* "Where are your credit cards' balances? Maxed-out or under control?"

* "Where will you take your first vacation when you succeed?"

* "Where was your last vacation, and is that good enough for you and your family?"

* "Where is the best place for your very first investment?"

* "Where would you like your first investment property to be located?"

"Why."

"Why" asks for an opinion. People love to give us their opinions.

"Why start working here at XYZ Corporation? We have the best facilities, the best research team, the best culture and the best salaries. Why not start here right away, and begin living the career of your dreams?"

***

"Why do you think it has taken so long to get to this point? The research has taken five years, the patent another five years, the government approvals five more years. Now this product is on the market and ready for you to go sell."

***

"Why spend all the time here today and go home with nothing? Take a free sample and fill in your email to get free updates. Make sure you have your name in the bowl for the lucky draw prize to win free products."

***

* "Why do you want to succeed so much?"

* "Why do people always say that today is the first day of the rest of your life? Because … it is."

* "Why is it that the best opportunities come when we have our biggest challenges?"

* "Why do you think I want to get this product in your hand right now?"

* "Why don't you start your new business tonight?"

* "Why not give it a go?"

* "Why not try it and see if you like it?"

* "Why not try a box today and see how you feel in a week?"

"How."

"How" sets a challenge to the audience. They will need to respond to this challenge. When you complete your presentation, it is time to take our talk to its natural conclusion.

"How we conduct ourselves in the community is a reflection on our values, beliefs and habits. How will you conduct yourself after this night?"

***

"How hard we work isn't a measure of success. The best way to measure success is by asking ourselves, 'Am I proud of what I do? Am I in love with my job and my career? How much do I love my job?'"

***

* "How excited are you about the weight-loss solutions presented tonight?"

71

* "How passionate were the speakers tonight?"

* "How can we get you started quickly?"

* "How can I help you build an international business?"

* "How can I help you retire early?"

* "How can I support you in this campaign?"

* "How will I know when you need me?"

* "How is the future looking now?"

* "How are you going to change the world?"

* "How will things change for you after you leave here tonight?"

* "How many people can you influence with what you know now?"

* "How many people are you going to share this information with?"

* "How can you help deal with this global issue at a local level?"

* "How can you make a difference in your neighborhood?"

* "How will the world be a better place because of you?"

* "How differently do you feel from when you arrived tonight?"

* "How do you feel about being able to retire in the next five years?"

* "How do you feel about being able to finally live your dreams?"

* "How will our lives change if we don't decide to move forward?"

* "How many people can now consider making a part-time income a reality?"

More short closes.

"Okay?"

Using the word "Okay" is a low-pressure close. We are just asking for them to agree, without any strong-arm tactics.

"Are you okay ...?"

* "Are you okay if we help you build this business?"

* "Are you okay with me helping you to get started right now?"

* "Are you okay with me being your coach?"

* "Are you okay with me holding you accountable to your goals?"

* "Are you okay with me building a strategy for you to succeed?"

"Is it okay ...?"

* "Is it okay with you if we finish the talk now?"

* "Is it okay if I tell you the truth?"

* "Is it okay with everyone if we finish on time?"

* "Is it okay for me to ask you to rate today's talk on a scale of one to ten?"

* "Is it okay to leave the excuses behind and focus on a positive future?"

* "Is it okay to start the next phase now?"

* "Is it okay if I write down the cost of getting started?"

* "Is it okay to give you the best price right now?"

* "Is it okay if tomorrow you start writing your blog?"

* "Is it okay with you to spend three more minutes on this topic, and then we can take a break?"

"Would it be okay …?"

* "Would it be okay for me to check if you are ready to invest?"

* "Would it be okay to start earning more money part-time than your old boss does full-time?"

* "Would it be okay to share a photo of me and my new book on your Facebook page?"

* "Would it be okay for me to autograph the books you buy tonight?"

* "Would it be okay for me to share with you the online resources we have?"

* "Would it be okay for someone to tell me the time?"

* "Would it be okay for you to post something about tonight's talk online, using #coachmarkdavis?"

* "Would it be okay for me to share your experience in a video interview after the talk?"

* "Would it be okay to write down a list of three people who you want to share this information with?"

* "Would it be okay to give the promoter a round of applause for putting tonight together?"

* "Would it be okay for you to pick up the order form in front of you and look at the #1 item?"

Rhetorical questions.

We can also ask a question that is rhetorical.

In our closing statement, we don't have to get an answer out loud. People may think about their answer and nod or shake their head.

We can prove our final point with a rhetorical question. It will relate to the material we have been talking about throughout our session.

Here are some examples.

* "It is time to make a change for yourself, to have the life you want, isn't it?"

* "When times are tough and you have the opportunity to change your own life, will you take it?"

* "You can turn it around, and your life will get better tomorrow, won't it?"

* "Where in the world has there ever been a better deal than today?"

"I wonder."

We can get our audience to think about the impact of the topic of our talk. Maybe they will think how our talk will affect other important people in their lives.

Some examples.

* "I wonder what your husband/wife/partner will say?"

* "I wonder what your husband will say when you are making an extra $1,000 a week?"

* "I wonder what your wife will say when you have saved $100 on your car insurance?"

* "I wonder what your accountant will say when your investment shows a 22% return?"

* "I wonder what your partner will say when you get an extra $5,000 back from your tax return?"

* "I wonder what your kids will say when you take them on that big holiday?"

* "I wonder what your wife will say when you show up with $2,000 cash for her to spend on whatever she wants?"

* "I wonder what your kids will say when you tell them they can go to private school?"

* "I wonder what your family will say when you announce your next vacation is in Europe?"

Assumptive closes.

Assumptive closes are the questions that get the audience to agree.

Assumptive questions tend to finish with an upward inflection in our voice. This invites the other person (or the audience) to respond. We are making a request of them to give an answer.

* "It is a great product, isn't it?"

* "Saving the oceans from pollution is good, isn't it?"

* "You do love your family, don't you?"

* "Want to give your family a vacation this year?"

* "Feel more energy already, don't you?"

* "Want that upbeat feeling every day?"

* "You can see how much money you need to retire now, can't you?"

"Isn't it time to upgrade?"

* "Isn't it time to upgrade your software to the latest version?"

* "Isn't it time to upgrade your phone so you can take advantage of smartphone technology?"

* "Isn't it time to upgrade your wardrobe to the 21st century so you can look modern and stylish?"

* "Isn't it time to upgrade your computer to a slim laptop from that slow and bulky anchor you are carrying around now?"

* "Isn't it time to upgrade your kids' schooling and give them more opportunities?"

* "Isn't it time to upgrade your restaurant choices to those that actually use proper tablecloths?"

* "Isn't it time to upgrade the hotels you stay at so you don't see another cockroach?"

* "Isn't it time to upgrade your vacation from the local beach to the beaches of Australia?"

"Don't you ...?"

* "Don't you want to feel better all the time?"

* "Don't you want to look younger and have people guessing your age?"

* "Don't you want to have passive income so that you work once and get paid forever?"

* "Don't you want residual income to keep coming in after the work is done?"

* "Don't you want a good, solid investment like all the people in the testimonials?"

* "You do believe me, don't you?"

* "You do trust me, don't you?"

Closing by introducing the next speaker.

If we are finished with our talk, we may have the job of handing over the floor to the next speaker. That means it is a good idea to know who is coming up next. Have a great introduction prepared, so the crowd will have with a good impression of us. Then the next speaker will come on stage feeling good about themselves. They will like you and remember that you handed them a positive, receptive audience.

"Well, my time is finished. You have been a great audience. I would like you to give a big welcome to our next speaker. He is a PhD, an all-around dating genius and also a nice guy. He is here to share with you why being intelligent can help you with your relationships. Please welcome Dr. Love to the stage with a big round of applause!!" (Start the clapping and wait on stage for the next speaker to come to the center stage. Then, quietly leave the stage in the background.)

***

"So thank you for having me here today. I have enjoyed my time sharing one of the pieces of the puzzle. For the next piece, you have a new speaker. She is the number-one salesperson of this product. She has created more customers than anyone on this planet. So get ready now to learn how to earn lots and lots of money. Please welcome Sharon Smith!"

How to hand over to the next speaker professionally with simple bridge phrases.

* "I am going to hand over the stage now."

* "Over to the next speaker."

* "In a minute, John will be taking over."

* "I can't wait for this next speaker. Wow! What an inspiration!"

* "Ready for something special?"

* "Here comes a bundle of energy!"

* "In the next five minutes, you will hear a story that will make you cry."

* "Our next speaker has 27 years of experience."

Feelings and emotions.

Our presentation can finish with us creating emotions and feelings for our audience.

Want a couple of examples of emotional endings?

"Yeah, and I love youse, too. I just also wanna thank God. Except for my kid bein' born, this is the greatest night in the history of my life. I just wanna say one thing to my wife who's home: 'Yo, Adrian! I did it!'"

— Rocky Balboa, *Rocky II*, 1979

"We will not go quietly into the night. We will not vanish without a fight. We're going to live on! We're going to survive! Today we celebrate our Independence Day!"

— Bill Pullman, *Independence Day*, 1996

"We choose to go to the moon. We choose to go to the moon in this decade and do the other things, not because they are easy, but because they are hard. [...] Because that challenge is one that we are willing to accept, one we are unwilling to postpone, and one which we intend to win, and the others, too."

— John F. Kennedy, 1962

"Do you remember?"

* How you felt when you watched a sad movie?

* When you fell off your bike and scraped your knee?

* When you smelled a fragrance in the department store

* When you got married?

* When your child was born?

All these events trigger emotional responses in our body. Some make us laugh, some make us cry. Others made us smile or even tremble with fear.

As a speaker, we can use emotions at the end of our talk. Getting the audience to feel something can help them make a decision. Emotions can strengthen the connection we have with our audience.

Remember, our presentation is just a story that other people will repeat tomorrow. Emotional stories get retold the most.

We can close and leave our audience with almost any feeling we want:

* Happy.

* Confident.

* Powerful.

* Motivated.

* Inspired.

All these make for great, positive ends to a talk. Other emotions for more dramatic endings could be:

* Challenged.

* Angry.

* Frustrated.

Let's work towards creating those emotions with our final words.

"Do you like me still?"

It is easier to close our talks when our audience is happy and they like us. Decisions are easier when everyone feels good.

Spending time at the beginning of our talk to build rapport is important. Emotional bonding with our audience makes us feel good also. But, we need to keep rapport all the way to our final words.

Some examples.

"I want to acknowledge those of you who had major breakthroughs. Thank you for sharing with the group. If you initially disagreed with the psychological methods we proposed, thank you for at least considering them. I respect your position. If anyone wants more time to discuss it in depth, I am honored to stay with you this evening so that we can talk in private."

"It has been great discovering the ways we can save our at-risk children tonight. We have more to learn and more work to do, but this was a great start. As I finish, please consider volunteering to help extend the reach of our mission. Please give me your volunteer form before you leave tonight."

"So after knowing Tom for all these years, it is great to see him be settled and … almost emotional! Even if it took him three years to plan his proposal, I am sure the next 30 years will be exciting and more spontaneous. Congratulations and good luck for your life together!"

"Thank you, thank you, thank you."

So what is the easiest way to get our audience to like us?

"Thank You."

This phrase works like a silver bullet to our audience's brain.

1. "Thank you" taps into the emotional and reactive mind. The part of the mind that feels. When we thank someone, they like us!

2. "Thank you" gives our audience feelings of acknowledgement. This helps our audience smile and be receptive to our close.

3. "Thank you" is a positive action we can take. This phrase taps into the childhood manners we were taught by our mother.

4. "Thank you" is short. It is a perfect close if we are running out of time and need a quick way to finish.

5. "Thank you" is universal. This phrase works everywhere in the world.

Saying "thank you" is a validation for the audience. It shows we are realizing that they are important to us. With this close, we speak to their ego. Yes, the audience is important.

Here are just a few ways we can say "thank you" to close our speeches.

"Thank you for your time."

Time is the most valuable resource for our audience. They invested their time, and will never get this time back. In return for their time investment, we have to produce value to reward their effort.

* "Thank you for listening to our presentation on the eight signs of aging and how to prevent them."

* "Thank you for listening to our talk on how to make an extra $2,000 a month in less than three hours a day."

* "Thank you for coming here today to learn how you can save over $175 on your car insurance."

"Thank you for your participation."

Sometimes we have an interactive program, a "hands-on" training or activity. Or, we asked our audience interactive questions and implemented exercises.

Games, exercises and challenges can take people out of their comfort zones. Maybe they got emotional and showed some vulnerability. It is good to thank the audience when they are breaking through personal barriers and showing people their softer side.

For their participation, we can thank them.

* "Thank you for volunteering tonight. It takes courage and you took yourselves out of your comfort zones. Congratulations on your personal breakthroughs."

* "Thank you for your participation. These events are successful when people like you get involved. I hope you can apply these exercises in your business and personal lives."

* "Thank you for completing the honest self-assessment of your financial position. Our 10-point wealth quiz shows your investing habits and mindset. Going forward, I hope you can see the possibilities for improving your net cash position."

"Thank you for your questions."

Some audiences ask questions and it is respectful for us to give them answers. Plus, with their issues resolved, they are more likely to act when we finish our presentation.

Some examples.

* "Thank you for all the questions on how to make more money and build a network. As our time is now up, any additional questions can be sent to our website."

* "Thank you for the questions on how to effectively travel overseas with your smartphone. I think everyone with a smartphone will have benefited. I appreciate your enthusiasm for travel!"

* "Thank you for asking questions about the ingredients in our new miracle skin cream. Now you have the latest information on this amazing product. Here is your chance to go out and sell our little miracle starting today!"

"Thank you for subscribing."

We often ask for a decision in our talks. We ask the audience to give their email address, phone number or payment details. We ask for trust from our audience. We should acknowledge that trust.

People can pull out their phone and can visit our website or registration page while we are talking. So when we clearly mention our website, our blog or our newsletter, we can make it easy for them to act right away!

Some examples.

* "My website is www.markdavis.com.au. Thank you for subscribing with your name and email. You will get access to my training resources, as well as news on upcoming books and seminars. Also, if you want, you can book me for speaking engagements or training calls."

* "My health and wellness blog web address is on the slide behind me. Thank you for subscribing today. For all new members, I have a $10 voucher. You can use the voucher towards free cappuccinos right here in the hotel."

* "My YouTube channel is the easiest way to follow my music videos. Subscribe there and I will thank you by sending you a special link. You can then download a free 'extended version' music video."

"Thank you for buying."

It is common courtesy when a customer buys something from us that we should say, "Thank you."

Thanking people at the point of sale, or even before the close, will plant a seed. Yes, thanking people in advance for their purchase is just as powerful as asking for the order when closing.

Some examples.

* "That is $179 for your kit. Thank you for your order."

* "It is just $99 to get started today, and you can pay by cash or credit card. Thank you in advance to those that know they want to get this starter travel package. Have you worked out when you plan to leave on your first mini-holiday with us?"

* "Thank you for considering my ideas on environmental waste reduction. Supporting these strategies is just $20 a month, and we can accept credit card payments now."

"Thank you for joining."

People like to join with others. This is why busy shops remain popular, and busy restaurants have a waiting list. It is good to acknowledge the valuable act of joining.

Joining is also infectious. Once one person joins, others tend to follow.

We can help our audience feel safe in joining by acknowledging their need to be with others.

Some examples.

* "Thanks for coming tonight to be part of the largest meeting on personal wealth creation in our city. I am

looking forward to hearing your success stories in the forums and at our meetings in the future."

* "Thank you for investing in your business by joining our community of health practitioners. It is the biggest in the Wide Bay region. Our network will enjoy having you as a new member. Remember, your business will immediately be placed in our directory."

* "Thank you for joining our group of like-minded entrepreneurs. Here at the Business Leaders Meetup, we will do all we can to help you find new customers. We look forward to your input at the monthly meetings."

"Thank you for paying attention."

This is a modern-era acknowledgement. With smartphones, it is easy for people to be distracted. If your audience has stayed away from their phones, thank them for paying attention. If your audience listened quietly through a long, boring presentation … thank them!

* "Thank you for paying attention during our movie. Now you know more about the environmental impact of plastic bottles dumped in the ocean. I know that you have a choice in your waste options. I know you will remember this movie when you make your decision to recycle in the future."

* "Thank you for paying attention to this vital topic of income diversification. The statistics are compelling and I could see many heads nodding throughout. Let's see how to get you started with XYZ investments."

* "Thank you for paying attention to our product demonstration. I believe that you have seen the first ever

LIVE instant facelift. The radical transformation happens in just 90 seconds. Do you want the same results at home? Come on over and order your product now."

The last speaker.

If we are the final speaker at a meeting, our talk should finish with "thank you."

After all the other closes, be sure to thank the following people:

* The organizer,

* The promoter,

* The person who introduced you,

* The person who spoke before you,

* The person who wraps things up after you, and

* The audience.

What happens when we thank other people who are in the room? It reminds the audience to clap. Most audiences are polite. And they have been trained to do this all their lives.

There are other things we can do to tap into different emotions in our crowd.

Remind our audience why they like us.

When we open our talk, we should say something designed to break the ice and make people like us.

Having them like us throughout our talk is important. We share our presentation, and the attention is on the content, not on us.

At the end of our talk, they must like us and trust what we said is true if they are to take action.

How do we build likability and trust?

Smile.

This is one of the simplest things we can do. Not enough presenters use the power of a smile.

We should smile before and during our closing statements. This is one of the most important basic body language tools.

* Smile at those people who interacted with us; those who nodded, smiled, and laughed.

* Smile at the people who asked us questions.

* Smile at the people who engaged with us.

* Smile at the people who volunteered.

* Smile at the people who didn't smile at you.

* Smile at the host.

Smiling is easy to do, and can be powerful. Our smile brings empathy and understanding.

What if it doesn't feel natural or easy? Here are a few tips to help.

1. In our notes, it is useful to draw the occasional smiley face. This will remind us to smile and will help us engage the audience. Because when we smile, they smile back. And if we get too serious, it will help lighten the mood.

2. We can prepare someone in the audience, preferably in the front row, to smile at us throughout our talk. We can ask for a volunteer in the front row before we begin our talk. Maybe we will get two volunteers! Whenever we look at them smiling at us, it will remind us to smile.

3. Before our talk, practice smiling! While we practice our speech, we should look at ourselves in the mirror. We can see what we look like when we smile.

Why is this important? Because there are many ways to smile and our smile needs to match its purpose. We want to engage people, not frighten them or creep them out!

We do not want to look like the Cheshire Cat from *Alice in Wonderland*. Or worse still, The Joker from *Batman*, or Jack Nicholson in *The Shining*.

Be real.

Everyone likes to believe that the performer at a concert is singing the song just for them. It is personal. The emotions are real, fresh and sincere.

Authenticity is a hard thing to fake because it is a feeling. We have to focus on being sincere so that our audience feels it too. It may be a performance, but it has to be real.

We should practice "thank you" statements. Just like the practice we did to create our perfect smile, we need our words to sound like we mean them! Sincerity, passion, happiness. We can communicate a lot with a smile.

Gratitude.

Being grateful for the chance to speak at a presentation should be sincere.

* "Thank you for having me, and I appreciate the opportunity. Speaking in front of a group of dedicated skincare professionals, I feel at home. I hope in some small way I have assisted you in selling more products and reaching your own sales goals."

* "It has been a real eye-opener to share my presentation with you today. Your knowledge of the topic has been second to none. You showed me this with the quality of the questions you asked. Today, I was able to share some new information because you are ready to add it to your knowledge bank."

* "I do not think I have ever had such an easy group to speak to. You loved my jokes. You interacted with my

questions and activities. And, you created a safe space for each other. That meant people could share their personal challenges with building a business. Thank you again for being such a supportive group."

When the audience feels our sincerity and authenticity, we have brought the talk to the perfect close.

What are some other magic sentence starters we can use? Something to express our authentic and sincere feelings without saying "thank you?"

"You have been ..."

These magic words help reinforce the rapport we have been building all through our talk.

When we refer to the past and what our audience has "been," they smile. They feel acknowledged. And it helps them focus on their personal feelings.

* "You have been a great crowd."

* "You have been a wonderful audience."

* "You have been the perfect group."

* "You have been asking some great questions."

* "You have been the most interactive trainees."

* "You have been laughing at all my jokes, I must really be funny!"

* "You have been paying attention and know all the answers now!"

* "You have been great partners for each other in the exercises."

* "You have been able to provide me with some great examples for my next talk."

* "You have been a great example of a motivated and energetic audience."

The audience feels positive, enthusiastic, and happy because they are focusing on what is most important to them: themselves!

They will see us as genuine and authentic. Plus, our audience will feel good about our talk.

Pick any emotion.

We can close our talk and have people feeling a particular emotion. This helps the audience make decisions instinctively.

Why do we want to use emotions in our close?

Because when we make a decision, we then associate the emotion we felt at the time. So if we feel strong emotions when we make the decision, we will always associate these strong emotions with that decision in the future.

For example, here is what people might remember about their decision after your presentation.

* "He seemed so friendly showing me that new red car and letting me sit in it ..."

* "She said I looked handsome, and I felt proud of all the fitness classes I had been taking ..."

* "I felt it was a trustworthy business with all the professional literature ..."

* "I just had so much energy after trying the product sample ..."

* "I felt like anything was possible and that they understood my personal goals ..."

* "There was a buzz in the air with so many people excited about losing weight ..."

* "The speaker was so amazing, I had to line up for 20 minutes just to get an autograph!"

When emotions are high, we make spontaneous decisions. And we will associate those emotions with our decision far into the future.

Let's look at some more examples of how we want our audience to feel.

Capable.

* Want the audience to take action on their diets? We want them to feel confident that they can stick with their plans.

* Want the audience to start their own business and make extra income? They need to feel that they have the skills and the support to learn how to do it.

* Want the audience to take on more responsibility in the company with a promotion into management? Let's help them feel capable with our presentation.

Safe.

* Want the audience to invest with us? They need to feel safe with the decision to hand over their money. We will need examples of other people who they trust that have made the same decision.

* Want the audience to try a new skincare product? They want to know it is not tested on animals and is going to be safe on their skin. Do we have the research and the proof? We will need it to show that it is safe.

* How about trying a new anti-aging product to make them look and feel younger? They want to know it is safe and will have no side-effects. Maybe show before-and-after photos, and also have testimonials from satisfied customers.

Happy.

Having the audience happy at the end of our talk is easy. We can encourage the audience to be happy by telling a final story about what we have been presenting. Stories of other happy customers or successes will be very effective.

When we share the highlights of our talk, we focus on the key learnings. Recapping the benefits helps the audience realize they are in the right place to benefit.

We also thank the audience and give them reasons to be happy and grateful that they attended. A simple thank you is always going to help people feel happy. We make them feel happy that their time was well-spent listening to us. This encourages a buying environment or a willingness to listen further.

* "It has been so much fun being here with you today. I look out and see all the smiling faces and it makes me happy. I hope you go home and hug your family and share this positive energy."

* "I am so happy to have been able to speak here tonight. I feel the bubbling, happy energy of this room, and I know this company is on the right track for success."

* "There is nowhere else I would rather be. I am happy to say this is the most fun I have had in a long time. You made this happen. And when you are happy, I am happy. Thank you."

Confident.

Confidence is that strong feeling that tells you that you can do it! You have proven you can do it, and you feel that can do it again.

The first time we try something new, we don't have confidence. Instead, we need to have trust and faith.

Reminding our audience of their newly-acquired confidence is a great way to finish.

* "Who would have thought when you walked in here a few hours ago, that you would be standing up and speaking? And in front of more than 40 people! Now you

can do it again and again. By the way, isn't the feeling of applause just awesome?"

* "Now you have a plan to grow your business by 100% in the next 6 months. I am here to help you, but I also know that you can do it. You have the ability and the skills."

* "You have seen how others have lost the weight and kept it off. You have the product to help get you there. You have the team around you to support you. We know you can do it, and you do too!"

* "Making money always looked difficult, but now you have the tools. You have set goals that you can achieve. You have a training and support team on hand to assist. And you have the self-motivation to break through any challenges along the way."

Successful.

The feeling of achievement is best created through a future-paced story. This means you will tell a story that puts people into the future 3-12 months.

Losing weight:

* "In three months, you will look back and realize that taking this first step was the beginning of a journey. A journey to more energy, better skin, and smaller clothes! You will enjoy better health, and the ability to walk up two flights of stairs without puffing."

* "You are going to inspire all those around you who have also had challenges with their weight. You will be a

mentor. You will help a lot of people. You will never be the same again!"

Or starting a business:

* "By following this plan for 12 months, your business will succeed. You can make more than $10,000 a month in residual income and have the freedom to quit your job and travel the world."

* "You have the goals you want to achieve. Maybe it is to earn your first $1,000 or to stand on stage at the international convention. Put those goals up on the wall, in your car, on your phone. Feel that sense of achievement like you have achieved it already!"

* "Starting a business is now the first step on your journey. You have achieved an amazing feat already. Soon you can fire your boss, work for yourself full-time, and then the sky is the limit!"

Or writing a book:

* "When you write those first 500 words tomorrow, you will feel a rush of adrenaline through your veins. The hardest part is beginning. Before you know it, you will be writing every day. You will be a writer! And it starts tomorrow."

* "In three months' time, you will have achieved the next major milestone with your story. Maybe your first draft will be completed. Then, you can start the editing, design the cover and start making sales! So don't give up. Keep writing!"

* "When you look back in a year and see five books in the bookstore, you will feel such a sense of achievement.

You will be a published author and have readers around the world. You will look back on today as the day it all began."

Satisfied.

* "Remember when you finished a big project for someone else in the past? You did the work and enjoyed the satisfaction of a job well-done. So now we have a project to work on that will double your satisfaction as you create something new that you own 100%."

* "Discipline is hard. Developing better nutrition and healthy habits is difficult also. However, next year your body will thank you. Start your adventure now."

* "When you partner with us, you will look back satisfied with the return on your investment. Your peace of mind comes from our strong management team, our low overhead, and successful past projects. Invest now with us, and stay within your comfort zone."

* "Satisfaction comes from knowing you did your best, and got a result that was equal to your time invested. Let's work to increase that, from feeling okay to feeling great. Let's go break some sales records together and make this product a household name."

Powerful.

Having power and exerting control are strong feelings. The lack of power often means people are making reactive decisions instead of proactive. Give your audience the chance to feel powerful and in control.

* "Getting to number one in sales with our company is a goal. Someone here will get there in the next six months. Then you have the power to determine when and where you work. When and where you vacation. You will be in control of your life."

* "Being the CEO is a role with a big responsibility. Responsibility gives you the power to affect the lives of everyone in the company in a positive way. To create the culture, and to maintain the direction we have started, we would like you to accept the position."

"Making an extra $2,000 a week will change your life. Now you have the power to pay your bills early, not late. The power to choose four-star hotels instead of two-star hotels. And finally, the power to tell your boss that you cannot work full-time anymore."

Angry or frustrated.

The emotion of anger needs to be well-focused. Do not direct it back onto the audience. They will get angry at us if we focus on their failures. We all have our reasons for past failures, but we need to direct their anger and frustration to a third party. It is important to have something else that they can be angry at. For example:

* Be angry at the government.

* Be angry at terrorists.

* Be angry at the buses and trains.

* Be angry at wasted time.

* Be angry at the education system.

In the brief moment, the anger will spur them into action to do something new. We offer them positive choices to channel and focus that angry energy.

At a workshop recently, I heard a speaker say, "Aren't you sick and tired of living in a poverty prison?" This was deliberate. He wanted the audience to use the imagery of themselves in prison. That would make anyone angry and direct the focus of their negative energy to his solution.

Stories of frustration turned to joy are a good way to finish. Our audience will put themselves into the story of challenge or frustration and will see hope from our story. They will feel exactly what the lead character in our story feels.

* "When I was sitting where you are today, I wished that I had gotten into property investing earlier. Frustration about my inaction drove me to come and listen. But I did act then. I got involved. Now that frustration is gone, and I own three condominiums by the beach."

* "Sitting there I know some of you have the frustration of not knowing what to do with your life. Today, let's move forward with a positive plan and a strategy to give you purpose and meaning."

* "As some of you might be thinking, you have been where I have been. Drowning on the bottom of the financial ocean. Filled with the frustration at your inability to get back above water. It is okay to take the time today to start researching new ways to change your life. Move ahead from old habits and old ways of doing business, into the new ways of the future."

We can motivate through frustration to get action from our audience. We want them to say, "Enough is enough!"

Match your words with your body language.

Emotions are important. Having sentences that trigger those emotions is important. However, our body needs to match the emotions we are seeking to elicit.

If we are feeling the emotion when we speak - they feel it too. When our body posture and gestures match - they feel it too.

When the volume we speak at and the speed matches our message - our audience will be feeling it too.

Want to show your feelings with body language?

* To be powerful, stand up straight and hold a strong posture. Use deliberate movements. Pause between sentences. Be loud enough and shake your hand at the audience with a closed fist. Make long eye contact with intensity.

* Want to look calm and cool and collected? We need to relax, smile, and use a softer tone of voice and smooth gestures.

* Motivated and excited and want to show it? We need to be loud! Fast! We should move around while telling stories.

Then, the audience will likely match our energy. And the buzz in the room will be wild!

More emotional closing statement starters.

Use these key words to start our closing statements. They help to generate an emotional response from our audience.

"I believe in you."

It is always nice to have someone else believe in us. It helps us to build our self-confidence and will increase our ability to act. Confidence comes from accepting that other people believe in us, so we can then believe in ourselves. Then, anything is possible.

* "I believe in you. Despite the reality of your past situations, the things that brought you down, you can do it. You can build your life again in the direction of your dreams. You can take control. There is a light at the end of the tunnel. And that light is your success shining towards you."

* "I believe in you. You can change your life and have energy levels beyond your wildest dreams. You have heard the stories of lives changed forever by taking this product. With more energy than ever before, improved memory, eyesight and cardiovascular capacity, you can do it all. The solution is here in front of you."

* "I believe in you. You can stand out from the crowd and be successful in a fulfilling career. If you want to stand out from everyone, you have to live today as if it were your last. You have to live with a passion like there is never going to be another weekend. Pour your heart and soul into everything you do. That is why we want you to come and work for us."

* "I believe in you. You can build a business! Working in the network marketing industry now is different than it was in the past. In our business, you have control. You have freedom. You have the ability to grow as far and wide as you want. You can travel the world with our business and see the amazing sights and sounds you have always dreamed of. Join our business today."

There is only one thing worse than taking action and making a mistake. What is worse? Never doing anything with our opportunity. Not doing is worse than doing and failing.

Avoiding regret comes from acting on our feelings in the moment and then learning to live with the consequences. So in our closing statements, we can take people into the future. Have them look back at today as being the day they made a good decision.

"When you leave here tonight ..."

* "When you leave here tonight, you will be happy that you joined. You now have the chance to express yourself as an entrepreneur. You have started your own skincare business and will help people look younger overnight."

* "When you leave here tonight, you will be glad you have these vitamins. You will go home wondering, "How did I ever live without these products? I want to help my eyesight, memory and energy levels so I look and feel younger!"

* "When you leave here tonight, you will be financially set up for the rest of your life. You can start a whole new life tonight for less than the cost of a cup of coffee."

* "When you leave here tonight, and go to bed excited, you will stare at the ceiling while thinking about the places you will go on your next vacation."

Looking back in the short term to a recent highlight is useful too.

"The best part of tonight was ..."

* "The best part of the talk tonight was learning how much we can save."

* "The best part of tonight was learning how much money we can make."

* "The best part of the meeting today was hearing that passionate story about Jenny finding her one true love."

* "The best part for me tonight was hearing the testimonials from Connie's happy customers."

* "The best part of the presentation was realizing that we can succeed if we know what to say and do."

* "The best part of tonight was learning the simple script that gives us the confidence to close our talk effectively."

* "The best part of the seminar was feeling the excitement that Peter showed when he delivered his speech without notes."

* "The best part of this workshop was all of us fulfilling our dream of standing and speaking in public with confidence."

* "The best part of this seminar should be the relief that we don't have to worry about our retirement anymore."

* "The best part of tonight was seeing you feeling the freedom you will have when you can quit your job!"

* "The best part of the board meeting for me was seeing our confidence in the future after reviewing the profit-and-loss statement."

* "The best part of this presentation is seeing you have peace of mind now that you have insured your cars and homes."

Remember, feelings are powerful. One of the biggest challenges for non-salespeople is getting people to buy. Feelings help your audience understand your passion for and belief in your offering.

Why do people buy at the end of our presentations?

* When people feel good, they buy from us.

* When people feel like they are going to miss out, they buy from us.

* When people feel like they could be the first, they buy from us.

* When people feel like everyone else has this product already, they buy from us.

* When people feel like this is their last chance for success, they buy from us.

* When we meet our audience's values with our product or service, they buy from us.

* When people feel like they could do this business and be successful, they join.

* When people feel like the insurance keeps their family safe in case they have an accident, they buy from us.

Need more reasons why our audience will agree or buy from us?

Think of what values people have and treasure. Some values could be:

* Safety and security.

* Freedom and pleasure.

* Success and power.

* Abundance and generosity.

All of these values create emotions. When we get a great emotional reaction from our audience, they will buy.

Emotions and feelings are good ways to link our closing statements.

But what about logic? Can we use logic to create an effective close to our presentation?

Logic doesn't have to be boring. In fact, the use of a logical close might be better for some of our talks.

This is important when emotion is seen as cheesy or sneaky.

Emotion vs. Logic.

Some examples?

* Emotional - "Buy this wonder product today and it will remove baldness forever!"

* Logical - "Our doctors have confirmed that this product stimulates the hair to regrow after just three doses. The 200 independent studies should be proof enough that you can start getting results now. "

* Emotional - "Join my business and you can send postcards to those skeptics who said you would never be successful in life."

* Logical - "With this strategy, you could duplicate the success of others currently in the same field. All this confidence comes from the proven results of 23 other clients. I encourage you to join."

Emotional statements can sometimes appear unbelievable or full of hype. Sometimes they don't match our personality. We want our audience to believe us. So using the right close that matches your style is important.

This is why the logical close is often more effective for some people. When we close with our preferential style, we get better results.

Professional closes.

When talking in certain professional settings, we might choose to end our speech with a logical, formal close that doesn't focus on feelings and emotions. We could choose:

* An ending that reviews the facts of our talk.

* Something which logically presents the benefit to the audience.

* A review of the key points so they can act without needing to ask questions.

A good time for this close could be:

* If you are selling multimillion-dollar properties.

* Balancing the budget at the company board meeting.

* Proposing a business venture to new prospects.

Logical, professional endings work well to "wrap things up" with facts and figures. They can help people justify their emotional decisions.

Audiences want to have the little voice in their head approving things. Imagine a small person ticking off boxes and saying, "Yes. It makes sense to proceed. Pull out your credit card now."

The facts.

Presenting the facts helps. More importantly, facts help justify the audience's decision that they have already made with their emotions.

Let's look at the facts ...

When emotions run high, we want to look at the facts. We need to bring the emotion to a manageable level. We want to re-engage the left brain, so the audience can logically agree with the idea being proposed. Once our audience is satisfied emotionally and logically, they can take the action we suggest.

* "Well, that was all very exciting, but as we close let's look again at the facts. The company is 17 years old. The managers have 50 years' combined experience. Their attitude is conservative. Your money is safe when invested with this company."

* "You have shared some strong emotions about your partner today. Let's look at the facts. Strengthening a relationship takes time and takes work on ourselves. Five sessions with the counsellor is recommended. You can book in with our receptionist today for your one-to-one consultation. We can do this together. You will not be alone on the journey."

* "Wow, amazing transformations today! Those instant facelifts were exciting to see but let's look at the facts. You need to have an ongoing beauty routine. Your diet needs to be well-controlled. You will need a month's supply of the product to test if it is going to work."

**Sometimes the best ending we can use ...
just makes sense.**

Tapping into the logical part of the brain is the key. It is a great way to let the rational mind have more input and control. Logic helps the mind agree with what we said.

When we argue with people, it is natural for them to put up barriers. Using a logical close to a talk is going to give us the best possible outcome.

* We emotionally engage our audience throughout our talk.

* We challenge, we inspire, we disturb, and we show hope.

* We make promises. We show them people losing weight, getting investment returns and changing their lives.

Now we can calm them down and strategically direct them towards making the decision that we want.

One way to do that is use the power of the past.

Recapping.

One of the best ways to close with cool, clear and calm logic is to recap our presentation. We might share the top three points from the presentation, and then give a solid, final closing statement.

* "So to recap, the yield on this investment over 5 years has been consistent, averaging more than 10%. This is a safe investment that performs well above market

expectations. We will continue to check on it and manage its growth daily. Your money is safe with us."

* "So to recap, the five people who had the skincare treatment tonight had some instant and amazing results. They look younger! The smiles on their faces show us how our appearance can affect our attitude. How fast do you want to look younger? It is up to you."

* "So to recap, this business model is proven internationally. People right here in your town have had success. Many have created part-time and full-time incomes working less than 20 hours per week. Your extra income can start as soon as you are ready to start. We are here to help and look forward to your success."

* "So to recap, having low energy will affect every area of your life. The product we showed you tonight will turn you around and give you superpowers! If you could increase your energy level just 20%, imagine how your productivity would skyrocket. How fast do you want that extra energy to kick in so you work faster and finish earlier?"

* "So to recap, the board has agreed that it makes sense to move forward. We will take advice on implementing new inventory management software upgrades. We approve staff pay increases of 1.4% and opening the Singapore office next year. Thank you for your attendance. The next meeting is September 1. This meeting is now closed."

* "So to recap, being unemployed isn't a decision, but rather a disturbing reality. Dealing with the reality means we must create more jobs for more people. We must start now to get additional government funding to expand our

outreach program. Let's work together with our resources to alleviate the chronic unemployment in our city now. I look forward to working with you and creating more jobs."

* "So to recap, your relationship problems feature you as the central player in this situation. Your history, your ethics, your beliefs and attitudes affect the way you behave. In the next relationship you have, remember that you are the primary factor. So be aware and keep working on yourself. Good luck and don't give up!"

* "So to recap, today you applied an acid peel. Then you applied two processes for moisturizing and rehydration. The facial massage has released toxins from below the surface. The products we recommend are available at the back of the room."

Want more ways to review the talk?

The following examples are ways we can close with a strong, clear statement. This will show that we know what we are doing, and we know what we are talking about.

Promises.

If we promise our audience a benefit in the beginning of our talk, then we should remind them that we delivered that benefit. We don't want our audience to forget our gift, do we?

* "When we started today, I said I would share with you the three secrets to good nutrition. Thank you for letting me share them with you. I am ready to take any questions you have now."

* "We opened today discussing the best way to invest in property in the current economic climate. Thank you for letting me share a few of my strategies. I appreciate your review of the research done by the XYZ Corporation. We want to help you find safe, secure investments."

* "At the beginning, we said we would show you how to take five years off your age with this miracle skin cream. Thank you for volunteering to try the product to see the difference it can make in just 90 seconds. Samples are available at the back of the room."

* "When we started tonight, the rain was falling and the wind was howling. Thank you again for coming out in this crazy weather. Thank you for taking the time to learn how to create a second part-time business. We know this will help you on the journey to financial freedom."

Challenges.

If we presented a challenge up front, you can now show how you solved that challenge. Then, you can thank them for participating.

* "When we opened tonight, I challenged you to find a way to add an extra $1,000 a month to your personal income. After looking at all the options out there, we have come up with two great ways to get that money and more. Thank you for your ideas, your feedback, and your openness on this topic."

* "The biggest challenge with personal health is the lack of supplements. We must find supplements that fit our personal nutritional needs and individual lifestyles. Thank you for sharing your health goals and what you

have tried previously. Here is your chance to try a new solution. Samples are available at the back of the room."

* "We opened tonight talking about the challenge for young people to get into the property market. With high prices everywhere, it can be hard to know where to start. Thank you for listening to my ideas on international property trusts. I believe they have helped open your mind to new possibilities. I hope we may help you gain your first investment property."

And if you opened with a question? Your ending should share the answer to that question. Now the answer seems so simple.

Learning.

Remind the audience what we learned during the talk. New information gives a strategic advantage in the marketplace. The reminder will add even more logical reasons to do business with us during our closing comments.

"Today we have learned how to ..."

* "Today we have learned how to build a bridge between two people. We used the conversational tools of mutual respect and empathy. We used listening skills and the mindset to be the best we can for our family. Going forward, we can all improve our relationships. This will give us a better quality of life. Thank you for participating and good luck building more bridges."

* "Today we learned how to write a headline, a sub-headline, and the first 4 lines of copy to get our readers to read our blog posts. Now it is time to look to the future. A future with lots of readers, lots of sales and lots of people interested in hearing what we have to say. Happy writing!"

* "Today we have learned how to start a conversation with anyone. Now we know the right questions to ask about their job. We know what to ask about their family, and what they like to do in their free time. During the break, or on the way home, start a new conversation. Good luck with your business!"

What other benefits can turn into a closing statement? Here are just a few ideas.

* Invest in the foreign exchange currency market with minimal risk.

* Create a Facebook ad campaign that brings you hundreds of new customers a month.

* Build a website from the ground up and attract new customers to it.

* Promote yourself in a Facebook group and get new fans to your own pages.

* Save $1,000 a year on your taxes.

* Make an extra $250 per day while you're sleeping.

* Find the best business investments in China.

* Get upgrades in five-star hotels every time you stay.

* Fly first-class at economy prices.

* Access the natural chemical in your brain that helps you concentrate.

* Find the best places for driving on the weekend with the top down on your car.

* Discover uncrowded beaches on the northern coast of Spain.

* Look younger in just minutes a day.

* Suppress our appetite with the basic building blocks of diet shakes.

It is worth taking the time to review the key benefits of your product. We can work these benefits into our closing statement.

Some examples?

"What we know now is ..."

* "What we know now is that property is a secure investment. Interest rates are low and attractive. Banks are willing to negotiate. You can get financing for your property today."

* "What we know now is that chocolate with high cocoa content is good for you. Chocolate is available in three types: white, milk and dark. There are chocolate samples in the back!"

* "What we know now is that coffee can be good for you. Coffee can be free if you tell others about it. Coffee can make you money. You can join our business and get some free coffee now!"

* "What we know now is that tax is not a one-dimensional topic. It is complex. There are over 12 legal

ways to minimize the tax you pay. Most basic tax advice is available for free when you book your free consultation with us today."

* "What we know now is that not all business models are the same. Network marketing is a very successful business model. Anyone can join a network marketing business. You can join today and build your own successful business starting ... now."

* "What we know now is that airline travel is safer than ever. Airline food is better than it was ten years ago. Flights are cheaper than they were 20 years ago. You can book a flight anywhere in the world right now."

No hype, no fluff, just sensible statements.

Using common sense, good logic and a good close will have our audience nodding, agreeing, and able to move forward.

Does this approach work for everyone? Are there more options?

Well, some just like telling others what to do. Let us look at the "instructions" closing technique.

How To End Our Speech
With Confidence

Instructions.

READER ADVISORY. This section is going to sound a bit bossy or aggressive. There is a good reason.

This method for closing a talk sounds a lot like we are telling people what to do. We are not asking, not suggesting, but telling our audience what we want them to do.

Some personality types don't like this approach. That is okay. We have already covered many alternative ways of ending our talks. This is just one method that has been successful for many speakers.

This section is about letting the audience know that we want them to act. We embrace the power of the stage and tell them exactly what we want them to do.

Ready for some examples?

It is time ...

* Okay, it is time to fill out the order form.

* Okay, it is time to choose. Let's place your product order.

* Okay, it is time to pull open that registration form in front of you and complete it.

* Okay, it is time to look at the price and see if it is right for you.

* Okay, it is time to ask ourselves some tough questions.

Why do instructions work?

Giving the audience an instruction or direction on what to do is easy. Why? Because by the time we get to the end of our talk, our audience is used to hearing us speak. Our expertise and authority means we have their respect and they will listen.

They trust us and will do what we say.

Instructional closes are a great way to have a predictable, logical ending to our talk. This is a finish to our presentation that gives the audience clear action steps.

The instructional close is great when the audience needs help to make a decision. When they need us to direct them, we must be open and tell people what to do. It is not the time for us to say, "Oh well, whatever."

And if we are selling, we want them to decide to buy, invest, enroll, join or subscribe … now.

Reminding the audience that "it is time" to make a decision brings reality home.

Give them a choice.

When we close, we might say:

"When you leave here today, you will do one of two things ..."

This helps people make a choice. Of course, either choice is okay. And both choices will work for you as the speaker. By giving them the choices, they feel they are exerting their free will. However, we stay in control by suggesting the choices.

We can give two or more alternatives for our audience. This is useful because it is efficient and quick. They already know what they want to do. We are just focusing their decision-making on limited choices.

The "alternative" choice ending helps us give our audience a simple choice between two options. We must phrase the close with our product benefit in it. The choices given should appear unbiased, but sometimes the choice is so obvious everyone will smile.

The choices need to make sense. The audience will choose one or the other. So use these key words in your close.

"So what is going to be easier for you?"

* "So what is going to be easier for you? Trying the skin cream and losing five years off your face instantly? Or keep looking old and wrinkly like your grandmother?"

* "So what is going to be easier for you? Trying the nutritional energy drink today? Or continuing the struggle for extra energy and being the first to go to sleep every night?"

* "So what is going to be easier for you? Downloading the kindle book online, or getting a paperback copy here tonight that I can autograph for you?"

* "So what is going to be easier for you? Reading the book while you ride the train to work, or listening to the audio in the gym?"

* "So what is going to be easier for you? Getting audios to play in your car or reading a book the old-fashioned way?"

* "So what is going to be easier for you? Getting the paperback books or the e-book versions?"

* "So what is going to be easier for you? Going home, or going to the lounge with your team and discussing what you learned tonight?"

* "So what is going to be easier for you? Grabbing a pen or grabbing a pencil?"

* "So what is going to be easier for you? Grabbing a pen to take notes, or trusting your memory?"

* "So what is going to be easier for you? Standing up and stretching, or standing up and shaking hands with someone next to you?"

Three choices ...

With three choices, there is nearly always one that fits for each audience member. High, medium or low. Hot, warm or cold. Three choices is a great number for getting decisions.

126

"You can ..."

* "You can write a list, discuss with a friend, or sit here and think it over."

* "You can fill in the registration paperwork, ask someone to help you do it, or bring it up to the front and we will do it together."

* "You can try a sample of our product right now, take a box home and try it for a month, or take home a dozen boxes and sell them to your friends for profit!"

Using a series of instructions can be useful to lead them step-by-step through a process. Order forms, registration documents, property contracts, or insurance applications will all need multiple instructions. We cannot expect people to perfectly fill in forms that they have never seen before.

"Now that it is time for me to finish, here is what I would like you to do."

Fill in the application form.

"We are going to fill in the application form. Start with your name, write clearly in capital letters if that helps. Email addresses and phone numbers are vital, and of course where you want the products shipped to in the address section.

"Choose the form of payment you want to use. When you are done, raise your hand and someone will come around to check that it is all correct. You now have a guaranteed order!"

Pull out your credit card.

"You will need to pull out your credit card now. Look at the front of it, with those raised numbers. Please fill in the form with just one of those numbers in each of the boxes. Be sure to put your expiration date in the right boxes, and the CVV or security code, which is on the back of your card in the white signature box. And then please sign the authorization. That will guarantee your order!"

Fill in the order form.

"To order this product, you will need to fill in the order form. Pay special attention to the quantity of each item. You don't want to get home and have 11 boxes of this product arriving when you only need one. Just enter the correct number clearly in the big yellow box.

"Then enter your shipping address and your payment details. The ordering team will process it tonight and we will ship your order in the next 24 hours."

Get your phone out.

"Pull out your smartphone and put the following reminders in your calendar for next Saturday:

* "Check through your online subscriber numbers and see how much they've increased.

* "Check your Facebook advertising and see the results your ads have created.

* "Check your PayPal account to see how many sales you have made."

Exercises.

We can instruct people with the statement, "We have one final exercise to do today." This will prepare them for the close, and ...

The audience relaxes.

They know it is nearly over, so now they can participate without stress. There won't be any more surprises. They don't have to think too much. And they don't need to be trying to work out why they are there. It is the end.

We are taking them down the home stretch.

The impact of these exercises can be magnified because of this relaxed state of mind. The audience has shifted and their attitudes are more receptive to instructions and suggestions.

So what are the best exercises to do in this limited amount of time that we have left?

Exercises that don't take long! We have to limit ourselves to something that will fill in the time, but have a definite end.

Examples of a finishing exercise?

* "In the last five minutes, I would like you to find a partner, and write down three things that each of you has learned. Share these discoveries with each other. After that, we will write down the top ten learnings from the group on the board, so you have more great notes to leave with!"

* "In the next five minutes, I would like you to form a group of four people and, one by one, share the thing you liked most in today's talk. Then, share how you are going to apply it when you leave."

* "In the last five minutes, please stand up and walk around the room. I want you to give your 30-second sales presentation for the 'Magic Skin Product' to five people. Share your new sales pitch, and get feedback!"

Quick commands.

* "Please grab your phone, and take a selfie with a big smile on your face! Are you going to post that right away?"

* "Please get your phone and take a photo of me. I will give you a few poses! Please tag me with #coachmarkdavis when you post it online, or send it to me!"

* "Please make a quick movie about today that is no longer than 10 seconds. Then post it on our Facebook page."

* "Please take a photo of your notes, because you don't want lose them!"

Writing.

Writing exercises are a good way to close your talk.

Make sure the audience writes something memorable and positive; it should also lead to some sort of action in your favor.

"Please write down ..."

* "Please write down the final draft of your speech. Then we are going to get you to practice it with a partner."

* "Please write down a list of the ten prospects you are going to contact tomorrow. Then try this new sales strategy with those prospects."

* "Please write down the name of the next city you want to travel to."

* "Please write down the number of new customers you will be working to get this week with your new presentation skills."

* "Please write down the number of presentations you are committing to do this week to reach your sales goals."

* "Please write down the number of personalized emails you are sending out tonight."

* "Please write down the goal for your income in the next 12 months."

Speaking.

Having the audience talk to each other is sometimes the best exercise. It is a way to close with participation and a way to bring the talk to a good end with good energy levels.

Talking to their partner, the person beside them, is a good way to let them "close" each other on your message.

As long as we deliver the instruction with respect and confidence, they will want to cooperate.

Using the word "please" is also a great softener for your instructions.

* "Please ask your partner to rate their confidence level now, on a scale of one to ten."

* "Please tell your partner the best thing you learned today."

* "Please ask your partner to summarize the fear they conquered tonight."

* "Please tell your partner your favorite success quote."

* "Please ask your partner which money-saving idea they are going to implement."

* "Please tell your partner the topic of the book you are going to write."

* "Please share with your partner your favorite phrase or quote from today's talk."

* "Please ask your partner what they will no longer procrastinate on."

* "Please tell your partner the number of new customers you want this week."

* "Please ask your partner about their goal for the next week."

Remember, this is not about being bossy or pushy. This is simply a clear instruction to take an action. Most audience members are happy to take directions from someone they trust.

The power of this method comes from our delivery, as audience members see us as a trusted professional.

And finally ...

Do you have a talk or presentation coming up soon?

When you finish your talk, you now have choices.

1. Are you going to use direct closing questions?

2. Will you offer two or three choices to the audience?

3. Will you use a quick one-line question to finish?

4. Will you stimulate, challenge or encourage your audience to act?

5. Do you have a feeling you want your audience to walk away with?

6. Do you have a lot of facts to end your talk so that people see value and will logically decide to buy from you?

7. Or do you just want to tell your audience what to do with a clear instruction?

The best part of this book is that there is no one right answer.

Every talk is unique. Every audience is different.

Our audience can respond to different endings. If we mix and match when we are preparing our talk, we might get a better result. Having a variety of methods is better than if we only have one.

I wish you the best on your journey to better public speaking.

Contact me anytime at mark@markdavis.com.au and visit http://www.MasterTheArtOfPublicSpeaking.com for free gifts, subscriber news and live speaking engagements.

You can also find our Public Speaking Mastermind group on Facebook for more support, ideas, coaching and networking.

All the best,

— Mark

OTHER SITES TO VISIT

When you want to simply watch great public speaking presentations, go to Youtube.com or Ted.com. Just about any good speech or talk is available on video so you can watch and learn how to improve your speaking.

One of the best ways to improve is to watch and listen to others.

You can order the book, *Public Speaking Magic*, to learn more about how to start your talks comfortably. I co-wrote this book with Tom "Big Al" Schreiter. The book is available directly from Amazon in Kindle, paperback and audio formats.

ABOUT MARK DAVIS

Mark Davis is an international speaker and trainer whose passion is to inspire people to grow, lead and connect.

His courses on public speaking have helped thousands of people across the world become more confident and more effective communicators.

Mark is also passionate about coaching, travelling and making a positive social impact.

Contact Mark at:

Mark@MasterTheArtOfPublicSpeaking.com

www.ingramcontent.com/pod-product-compliance
Lightning Source LLC
Chambersburg PA
CBHW051319170526
45166CB00002B/609